T0063334

THE MESSIAH HAS RISEN

HEGNAL S. DAWSON

WestBow®
PRESS
A DIVISION OF THOMAS NELSON
& ZONDERVAN

Scripture taken from the King James Version of the Bible.

WestBow Press books may be ordered through
booksellers or by contacting:

WestBow Press
A Division of Thomas Nelson & Zondervan
1663 Liberty Drive
Bloomington, IN 47403
www.westbowpress.com
1 (866) 928-1240

ISBN: 978-1-4908-4728-3 (sc)

Library of Congress Control Number: 2014913995

Printed in the United States of America.

WestBow Press rev. date: 10/15/2014

THE AIM OF THIS BOOK:

To inform you that of a truth Jesus The Christ is the Son of God, As it has been pointed out in the King James Version of The Holy Bible. He is real. He lived on this earth. He is the Messiah The Promised One. His life on this earth was a sacrifice for the redemption of mankind. Because of him mankind may live without any possibility of death any more. If you accept Jesus as your Savior from the penalty of your unrighteous deeds through faith from the teaching of his holy word you shall be save.

The aim above to write this book was so clear. It became evident that the Holy Spirit was instrumental in reminding me of various texts at the most appropriate times.

Part edited by: Pastor, Dr. Fitzroy Maitland

Encouragement by: Pastor O.S. Phillips

Cover artistry by Dwight Brown, Eng.

The Messiah said:

"He that believeth and is baptized shall be saved; but he that believeth not shall be damned" (Mk.16:16 KJV)

The following questions are all answered in the texts that follow. Please fill in the appropriate blanks:

Do you know where Jesus lived during the last three and one half years while being here on earth?

1. *"And leaving Nazareth, he came and dwelt in Capernaum, which is upon the sea coast, in the borders of Zabulon and Nephthalim:"* (Matt.4:13 KJV)

2. What are some of the things he did while he was here?

   a. Heal the sick.

   b. Raised some-one from the dead.

   c. Taught the will of his Father through sermon, performed miracles and the life he lived.

   d. All the above?

3. Name some of his relatives while he was here on earth? Is not this the carpenter's son? Is not his mother called _____? And his brethren, _____? _____, and _____, and _____? (Matt. 13:55 KJV)

4. What happened to him? He was _____. "When the chief priests therefore and officers saw him, they cried out, saying, *Crucify him, crucify him,* Pilate saith unto them, Take ye him and *crucify him:* for I find no fault in him." (Jn. 19:6 KJV)

5. He was buried and then rose from the dead the 3rd day. What's the name of the day he was crucified according to the Jews? _____ _____." The Jews therefore, because it was the preparation, that the bodies should not remain upon the cross on the Sabbath day, (for that Sabbath day was an high day,) besought Pilate that their legs might be broken, and that they might be taken away". (Jn. 19;31KJV) (another fact) "Now in the place where he was crucified there was a garden; and in the garden a new sepulchre, wherein was never man yet laid. There laid they Jesus therefore because of the Jews' preparation day; for the sepulchre was nigh at hand.

6. On what day of the week he was risen? _____." The first day of the week cometh Mary Magdalene early, when it was yet dark, unto the sepulchre, and seeth the stone taken away from the sepulcher" (Jn.20:1,KJV) "In the end of the Sabbath, as it began to dawn toward the first day of the week, came Mary Magdalene and the other Mary to see the sepulchre." (Matt.28:1KJV) "Now upon the first day of the week, very early in the morning, they came unto the sepulchre, bringing the spices which they had prepared, and certain others with them." (Luke24:1 KJV)

7. Where is he now? _____. "He that descended is the same also that ascended up far above all heavens, that he might fill all things." (Eph.4:10 KJV) "And when he had spoken these things, while they beheld, he was taken up; and a cloud received him out of their sight. And while they looked stedfastly toward heaven as he went up, behold, two men stood by them in white apparel;" (Acts 1:9, 10 KJV)

8. Who is he now? Or what is his portfolio now? _____ Seeing then that we have a Great High Priest, that is passed into the heavens, Jesus the Son of God, let us hold fast our profession. For we have not an high priest which cannot be touched with the feeling of our infirmities; but was in all points tempted like as we are, yet without sin." (Heb.4:14,15.KJV)

Jesus is now our Great High Priest in heaven. He represents all who believe in Him as the Messiah and accepts him as our Savior and Lord by affirming it as we do the will of Our heavenly Father through the faith we exercise in Him.

9. What is he doing for those who believe in him? _____ Jesus said to his disciples; " And if I go and prepare a place for you,

I will come again, and receive you unto myself ; that where I am; there ye may be also." (John 14:3 KJV)

Preparing a place for those who believe he is the Messiah, The lamb of God who taketh away the sin of the world.

10. Will we see him again? _____ Which also said, "Ye men of Galilee, why stand ye gazing up into heaven? this same Jesus, which is taken up from you into heaven shall so come in like manner as ye have seen him go into heaven." (Act 1:11,KJV) "For the Lord himself shall descend from heaven with a shout, with the voice of the archangel, and with the trump of God: and the dead in Christ shall rise first: Then we which are alive and remain shall be caught up together with them in the clouds, to meet the Lord in the air: and so shall we ever be with the Lord." (1 Thess. 4:16,17 KJV)" Behold, he cometh with clouds; and every eye shall see him, and they [also] which pierced him: and all kindreds of the earth shall wail because of him. Even so, Amen." (Rev.1:7 KJV)

Please note; This book was written, bearing in mind, those who may not have a copy of the Holy Bible at hand. To those with a copy of the Holy Bible, you have the right to check your Bible along while you read. If you do not have a copy of the Holy Bible and you would like to have one you may write to us and request one. (King James Version) available to the first twenty (20) buyers for up to three years.

Answers:

1. Capernaum
2. D (a. Jn. 4:50 KJV) (b. Jn. 11:40-45KJV) (c. Matt. 5-7:1-29KJV) (Jn. 5:19-21KJV)
3. Mary, James, Joses, Simon and Judas
4. Crucified
5. Preparation Day
6. 1st Day of the week
7. Above all the heavens
8. Great High Priest
9. Preparing a place for us
10. Yes

CONTENTS

pages

THE LIVING WORD

St. John 1:1-3 KJV) Says:

"In the beginning was the Word, and the Word was with God, and the Word was God.

The same was in the beginning with God.

All things were made by Him; and without him was not any thing made that was made." (Jn.1: 1-3 KJV)

The Bible declared that Jesus was " The Word" before he took on flesh and became man. The book of Genesis describes creation in action. As states " And God said 'let there be… and it was made…and it was very good.' " (Gen 1: 3,6,9,11,14,20,24 KJV)

Jesus is truly God and He is truly Man. The scripture said: "And a certain scribe came and said unto him, 'Master I will follow thee wheresoever thou goest . And Jesus saith unto him, The foxes have holes, and the birds of the air have nests; but the Son of man hath not where to lay his head." (Matt. 8: 19,20 KJV). –

"And when he was come to the other side in the country of Gergesenes, there met him two possessed with devils, coming out of the tombs, exceeding fierce, so that no man might pass by that way. And, behold, they cried out, saying, 'What have we to do with thee, Jesus, thou

Son of God? art thou come hither to torment us before the time? '"(Matt 8:28,29 KJV)

These two scriptural passages states two titles of who Jesus was while being here on earth.

Please note who said these words.

Jesus declared himself to be the Son of man

while the devils identified him "Jesus, thou Son of God"

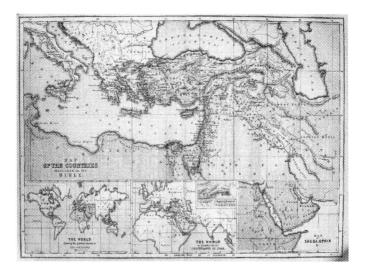

The devils also acknowledged that Jesus had the power to torment them and such stated that there is a determined time for this torment. Would this time be after the judgment? What judgment? Paul the Apostle said:

"In the day when God shall judge the secrets of men by Jesus Christ according to my gospel". (Rom. 2:16 KJV.)

"For the Father judgeth no man, but hath committed all judgment unto the Son. That all men should honor the Son, even as they honor the Father. He that honoreth not the Son honoreth not the Father which hath sent Him." (Jn. 5: 22,23 KJV)

". And he said unto them, Ye are from beneath: I am from above: ye are of this world: I am not of this world. I said therefore unto you, that ye shall die in your sins: for if ye believe not that I am he, ye shall die in your sins." (John 8:23-24.KJV)

Jesus Christ is to be recognized, acknowledged, and accepted as the Son of God. Creator and likewise, Savior of the world. The Messiah, the Anointed One.

In writing about the passage Matthew 8: 28,29 after I read and made these notations I stopped. And on attending service the following morning, I heard the Pastor referred to this passage and gave some details about it which just coincided with what I wrote. I give God the Praise knowing how He can use one to convey a message at the right time. As it is said often times in the church I attend, Whoever comes to church by what ever means does not come by chance but comes according to God's appointment.

I said that because the word of God does not and will not go void. Although that was not the sermon that was originally intended to be preached as was stated by the preacher and likewise noted in the bulletin for that day.

NAMING A CHILD OR CHANGING A NAME

In a bible lesson guide I read under the caption What's In a Name? "Names were very important in the biblical world. A name told of the person's cultural heritage and beliefs or pointed to the wishes of the parents of the child. Often a change in life circumstances or beliefs was indicated by a change of name". And three names were cited, Abram (Gen. 17:5KJV) Jacob (Gen. 32:27,28KJV) and Daniel (Dan.1:7KJV).

"SDA Church Adult Sabbath School, Bible Study Guide, page 50, Nov. 3rd, 2010."

How truthful is this . This study will cite to Matt, 1:21KJV more than once to keep things in context.

"But while he thought on these things, behold, the angel of the LORD appeared unto him in a dream, saying, Joseph, thou son of David, fear not to take unto thee Mary thy wife: for that which is conceived in her is of the Holy Ghost. And she shall bring forth a son, and thou shalt call his name JESUS: for he shall save his people from their sins. Now all this was done, that it might be fulfilled which was spoken of the Lord by the prophet, saying, Behold, a virgin shall be with child, and shall bring forth a son, and they shall call his name Emmanuel, which being interpreted is, God with us. Then Joseph being raised from sleep did as the angel

5

of the Lord had bidden him, and took unto him his wife:"(Matt. 1:20-24 KJV)

Here the angel of the Lord appeared unto Joseph. A man who was the espoused husband of this virgin in the lineage in which is prophesied in Isa. 7:14 KJV "Therefore the Lord himself shall give you a sign; Behold, a virgin shall conceive, and bear a son, and shall call his name Immanuel.**"**

This Joseph was an offspring of Jacob. "And Jacob begat Joseph the husband of Mary, of whom was born Jesus who is called Christ" (Matt.1:16.KJV) Jacob was a man whose name was changed to Israel, the Father of the children of Israel.

You will remember that it was said before, that names were very important in the biblical world. A name told of the person's cultural heritage and beliefs or pointed to the wishes of the parents of the child.

"And she shall bring forth a son, and thou shalt call his name JESUS: for he shall save his people from their sins". (Matt.1:21.KJV) Scripture gives the reason for him to be named Jesus

"He shall save his people from their sins." Who gave him this name Jesus (Savior)? His Father –The Almighty God who informed Joseph through an angel in a dream.

In the book of Acts 2: 22 KJV)one of Jesus' disciples said to a multitude of people on a specified-day. "Ye men of Israel, hear these words; Jesus of Nazareth, a man approved of God among you by miracles and wonders and signs, which God did by him in the midst of you, as ye yourselves also know:" At the same meeting, Peter continued speaking as he said:

"Therefore let all the house of Israel know assuredly, that God hath made the same Jesus, whom ye have crucified, both Lord and Christ. Now when they heard this, they were pricked in their heart, and said unto Peter and to the rest of the apostles, Men and brethren, what shall we do? Then Peter said unto them, Repent, and be baptized every one of you in the name of Jesus Christ for the remission of sins, and ye shall receive the gift of the Holy Ghost. For the promise is unto you, and to your children, and to all that are afar off, even as many as the Lord our God shall call." (Acts 2:36-39 KJV).

Jesus, Jeshua, (Greek) What more do you know about that Name and the person? The Name Jesus meaning "Jehovah is salvation" identifies the person. We note that there was none other who was able to do the work that this Jesus the Son of God did. Jesus, the individual, the sacrificial lamb who paid for our redemption, the anointed one "who has sacrificed his life for the redemption of his people from their sins. Paul says:" Let this mind be in you, which was also be in Christ Jesus: who, being in the form of God, thought it not robbery to

7

be equal with God: But made himself of no reputation, and took upon him the form of a servant, and was made in the likeness of man: And being found in fashion as a man, he humbled himself, and became obedient unto death, even the death of the cross. Wherefore God also hath highly exalted him, and given him a name which is above every name: That at the name of Jesus every knee shall bow, of things in heaven, and things in earth and things under the earth; And that every tongue should confess that Jesus is Lord, to the glory of God the Father". (Phi.2:5-11 KJV)

Every knee shall bow giving allegiance to "Jesus the Son of God" who gave all for the redemption of mankind. The day will come when even the dead after the resurrection will bow their knees before Jesus our Savior and Lord. The Judge of all judges, and King of all kings.

Have you heard or read the story about Nebuchadnezzar who had set up in the plain of Dura a golden image? Read (Dan. 3: 2-6 KJV) "Then Nebuchadnezzar the king sent to gather together the princes, the governors, the captains, the judges, treasures, the counsellors, the sheriffs, and all the rulers of the provinces to come to the dedication of the image which Nebuchadnezzar the king had set up. Then the princes, the governors, the captains, the judges, the treasures, the counsellors, the sheriffs, and all the rulers of the provinces were gathered together unto the dedication of the image which Nebuchadnezzar the king had set up; and they stood before the image that Nebuchadnezzar had set up. Then an herald cried aloud, To you it is commanded, O people, nations, and languages, That at what time ye hear the sound of the cornet, flute, harp, sackbat, psaltery, dulcimer, and all kinds of musick, ye fall down and worship the golden image that Nebuchadnezzar the king hath set up: and whoso falleth not down and worshippeth shall the same hour be cast into the midst of a burning fiery furnace."

Can you imagine the number of people that were there? A place where there were so many officials, the king and his honored statue? Well my friends even so many times greater shall the number bow before Jesus the Almighty Judge.

"A fiery stream issued and came forth from before him: thousand thousands ministered unto him, and ten thousand times thousand stood before him: the judgment was set, and the books were opened " (Rev.7:9-10 KJV) For more ; And when he had taken the book, the four beasts and four and twenty elders fell down before the lamb,, having every one of them harps, and golden vials full of odours, which are the prayer of saints. And they sung a new song, saying, Thou art worthy to take the book, and to open the seal thereof: for thou wast slain, and hath redeemed us to God by thy blood out of every kingdred, and tongue, and people, and Nation; And hast made us unto our God kings and priests: and we shall reign on the earth. And I beheld, and I heard the voice of many angels round about the throne and the beasts and the elders: and the number of them was ten thousand times ten thousand, and thousands of thousands; Saying with a loud voice, Worthy is the Lamb that was slain to receive power, and riches, and wisdom and strength, and honour, and glory, and blessing. And every creature which is in heaven, and on the earth, and under the earth and as such are in the sea, and all that are in them, heard I saying, Blessing, and honour, and glory, and power, be unto him that sitteth upon the throne, and unto the Lamb for ever and ever. And the four beasts said, A-men. And the four and twenty elders fell down and worship him that liveth for ever and ever." (Rev.5:8-14 KJV)

In (Matt.28:18 KJV) The scripture also reads of Jesus saying "all power is given unto me in heaven and in earth. " A man yet God who has infinite power, yet humbled himself while being here on earth even to his subjects whom he created.

"Be it known unto you all, and to all the people of Israel, that by the name of Jesus Christ of Nazareth, whom ye crucified, whom God raised from the dead, even by him doth this man stand here before you whole. This is the stone which was set at nought of you builders, which is become the head of the corner. Neither is there salvation in any other: for there is none other name under heaven given among men, whereby we must be saved. " (Acts 4:10-12 KJV)

Here, this passage is saying, that through no other source or person would one be able to be saved except through JESUS the CHRIST. The Name that was given above every other name which identifies the Creator, Savior, Redeemer, provider, etc. and friend of all.

From what is written, "thou shalt call his name 'JESUS' for he shall save His people from their sins." (Matt. 1:21) Jesus the Christ was the one who sacrificed his life on Calvary's cross for our redemption. We realized our redemption only after we have accepted what he has done for us. He gave his life on the cross for us at Calvary. It is only his blood can cleanse us of our sins. Nothing-else but his blood. From what was declared, the question must be asked, will the name Jesus cleanse our sins? Through the name Jesus, we can be led to be cleansed from our sins by the application of his blood through him who is now our High Priest.

"Wherefore he is able also to save them to the uttermost that come unto God by him, seeing he ever liveth to make intercession for them. For such an high priest became us, who is holy, harmless, undefiled, separate from sinners, and made higher than the heavens; Who needeth not daily, as those high priests, to offer up sacrifice, first for his own sins, and then for the people's: for this he did once, when he offered up himself." (Heb.7:25-27 KJV)

"But Christ being come an high priest of good things to come, by a greater and more perfect tabernacle, not made with hands, that is to say, not of this building; neither by the blood of goats and calves, but by his own blood he entered in once into the holy place, having obtained eternal redemption *for us.* For if the blood of bulls and of goats, and the ashes of an heifer sprinkling the unclean sanctifieth to the purifying of the flesh: How much more shall the blood of Christ, who through the eternal Spirit offered him self with out spot to God, purge your conscience from dead works to serve the living God?" (Heb.9:11-14 KJV)

The person Jesus acknowledges all who truly believe in him as the Son of God, who is our Savior. The conveyance of our desires by the Holy Spirit makes our requests known to his Father. At the mention of the name Jesus, our everlasting Father hears and responds on behalf of His Son, Jesus Christ our Savior in accordance to His will. Our everlasting God knows our needs. He answers according to His will. We are all His sons and daughters, initially as a matter of fact, but only One begotten Son, and that is Jesus the Christ. . The Name Jesus is not just a conduit, channel or only an identifier. By calling upon his Name Jesus (the same Jesus of Nazereth) you could receive God's saving grace, comfort, peace of mind, etc..

The name Jesus identifies the Person, the begotten son of the Father who stands in the gap for us. His name is also his nature to save. He is our " Great High Priest." (Heb. 4:14 KJV) One comes to God the Father through the intercessory work of his Son Jesus who "takes away the sin of the world." (Jn.1:29 KJV). Jesus said unto him,

"I am the way, the Truth, and the life: no man cometh unto the Father, but by me." Also - "But when the Comforter is come, whom I will send unto you from the Father, even the Spirit of truth, which proceedeth from the Father, he shall testify of me." (Jn.14:6, & 15:26 KJV)

AFTER JESUS' CRUCIFIXION

Prior to the announcement and declaration by Peter to accept this Jesus who was the Messiah and who had caused the experience on the Day of Pentecost, there was not a general concern by the public about the name Jesus the Christ. About the person, yes. There was also some concerns about some of what he had done and likewise about who he said he was while being here on earth.

Scripture said, Peter told the people on the day of Pentecost . But Peter, standing up with the eleven, lifted up his voice, and said unto them, "Ye men of Judaea, and all *ye* that dwell at Jerusalem, be this known unto you, and hearken unto my words: For these are not drunken, as ye suppose, seeing it is but the third hour of the day. But this is that which was spoken by the prophet Joel; and It shall come to pass in the last days, said God, "I will pour out my Spirit upon all flesh: and your sons and your daughters shall prophesy, and your young men shall see visions, and your old men shall dream dreams: And on my servants and on my handmaids I will pour out in those days of my Spirit; and they shall prophesy: And I will show wonders in heaven above, and signs in the earth beneath; blood, and fire, and vapour of smoke: The sun shall be turned into darkness, and the moon into blood, before that great and notable day of the Lord come: And it shall come to pass *that* whosoever shall call on the name of the Lord shall be saved." (Acts 2:14-21 KJV)

"Therefore let all the house of Israel know assuredly, that God hath made the same Jesus, whom you have crucified, both Lord and Christ. Now when they heard this, they were pricked in their heart, and said unto Peter and to the rest of the apostles, men and brethren, what shall we do? Then Peter said unto them, Repent, and be baptized every one of you in the name of Jesus Christ for the remission of sins, and ye shall receive the gift of the Holy Ghost." (Acts 2:36-38 KJV)

Peter's response was done in the presence of different representatives of various nations consisted of both Jews and Gentiles. Was Peter suggesting or implying that, those individuals or the mass of people who did not believe who Jesus was while he was here on earth, should now accept and or acknowledge the name of "Jesus Christ" as Savior and Lord but ignore the person Jesus and the ministry he presented? Remember Jesus was not accepted by the majority of the people, and that even still applies today. Peter stated this to the people that they would believe in this Jesus the Christ who presented this Gospel of his Father which declared that he Jesus is truly the Messiah. In believing this message and taking the necessary steps, then truly by faith those who believe would receive the promises stated.

Paul, Silas and Timothy, earnest believers in Jesus were faced with this question also "Sirs, what must I do to be saved? "Paul said "Believe on the Lord Jesus Christ, and thou shalt be saved, and thy house. And they spake unto him the word of the Lord, and to all that were in the house. And he took them the same hour of the night, and watched their stripes; and was baptized, he and all his, straightway. And when he had brought them into his house, he set meat before them, and rejoiced, believing in God with all his house. " (Acts 16:31-34 KJV) Paul the teacher informed this man and his household in who they should believe, The Lord Jesus Christ. Not only in his name but also the person.

I bought a " Nelson King James Version Study Bible. (previously published as The Liberty Annotated Study Bible and as The Annotated Study Bible, King James Version) Concordance copyright 1981 by Thomas Nelsen, Inc. On the cover it states "The Most comprehensive KJV study Bible ever Published.

Relating to Acts 2:38.KJV This is the commendation: **Repent** means "to change one's mind." Here as throughout scripture, one aspect of conversion is commonly used to represent all aspects: Believing and calling as well as repenting. The grammatical name for allowing part of something to represent the whole is called synecdoche. Repentance is something every person must do (17:30) For several reasons be baptized should not be joined with for the remission of sins to teach baptismal regeneration. First the context of this passage demonstrates that only the repentance is connected with the removal of sin at salvation; "Whosoever shall call … shall be saved"(v.21). Peter's next recorded sermon states only: "repent…that your sins may be blotted out" (3:19). Second, throughout Acts men demonstrate their faith and salvation prior to baptism (cf. 10:43-47). Third, the soteriological passages throughout the New Testament do not include water baptism in the salvation experience – John 3:16: Acts 16:31: Romans 4:10;Ephesians 2:1-10; 1 Peter 1: 18,19. Thus this verse more clearly reads, "Repent for the remission of sins, and you will receive the gift which is the Holy Sprit; and let each of you be baptized in the name of Christ." Though water baptism does not save you or wash away our sins, it is a command that needs to be obeyed speedily after conversion. Jesus commanded it (Matt 28:19,20), as does Peter here. This is the consistent pattern throughout Acts (16:31-34; 18:8).

Christ: The title of Jesus, the Anointed One, Savior: the Messiah. The fulfiller of all prophecies relating to him as the Messiah. "Therefore the Lord Himself shall give you a sign; Behold a Virgin shall conceive, and bear a son, and shall call his name Immanuel; (Isa 7:14 KJV) During Jesus' earthly ministry he declared who he represented. " I come down from heaven, not to do mine own will, but the will of him that sent me "(Jn.6:38 KJV.) "I can of my own self do nothing; as I hear, I judge; and my judgment is just; because I seek not mine own will; but the will of The Father which hath sent me." (Jn. 5:30.KJV)

Towards the end of his earthly ministry in the Garden of Gethsemene scripture records, " And he went a little farther, and fell on his face, and prayed, saying, O my Father, if it be possible, let this cup pass from me: nevertheless not as I will, but as thou wilt." (Matt. 26:39.KJV)

Here Jesus declared that he was on a mission for his Father. He lived as his Father would have him to have lived. He healed the sick, raised the dead, give sight to the blind, feed the hungry, taught his Father's will to the people and no less He himself lived an exemplary life to demonstrate that what his Father requires of mankind we too can accomplish same.

We must first seek the help of him, Jesus of Nazareth the Son of the living God. This Savior who left all his majesty above, humbled himself and became a lowly human being.

The Savior, of the world was predestined before the foundation of the world to save mankind from the penalty of sin which is death. He came into the world at the right time via the channel of humankind through a virgin named Mary. He was distinctly named "JESUS" because He came to save his people from their sins. Other names he received " Emmanuel" meaning God with us. "Son of God" that's who he truly was. "Son of man" a man born of a woman. "Michael ", and his angels fought against the dragon; and the dragon fought and his angels," (Rev. 12:7 KJV) He learnt a trade, carpentry, from which the family could make a living. The son of man suffered in various ways even from his own fellowmen. He got tired, He slept in a boat, he defended his Father's property, the house of prayer, etc.…

The expectation of who this Messiah should be was so great that religious leaders of the day could not accept such a humble, lowly man, who was well known by the people.

The question is, how could this Jesus be the Messiah who the people of the day sought? He walked, spoke, ate and drank with the people of various state of life. Unlike any other of such acclamation. Under such simple conditions the religious leaders and people wouldn't accept him as the expected Messiah. Yet he did all the things that were foretold of this Messiah to come.

In John 14:10,11KJV, it says, "believest thou not that I am in the Father, and the Father in me? The words that I speak unto you I speak not of myself: but the Father that dwelleth in me, He doeth the works, Believe me that I am in the Father and the Father is in me: or else believe me for the very works' sake**."** Here Jesus declared himself plainly his relationship with his Father and his Father's relationship with him. And if you fail to understand, he declares, "believe me for the very works' sake. " No one had ever done all of what he had done.

Here, even his works testified of him to give a simpler understanding to both the intellectuals and to the simple minded that they had no excuse or reason to say he had not accomplish the expectation as the Messiah. Even today, the opportunity is still available for accepting Jesus as the Messiah, as your Savior and Lord.

Will you? _____ or have you? _____

GOD'S LOVE EXPRESSED THROUGH JESUS CHRIST HIS SON, OUR SAVIOR

In the scriptures it is told that there would be a Savior who would come to save His people from their sins. That includes both you and me. It was foretold of Jesus before he was manifested in the flesh :

Why? As we have learnt "wherefore, as by one man sin entered into the world, and death by sin; and so death passed upon all men, for that all have sinned." (Rom.5:12KJV)

"For God so loved the world, that he gave his only begotten Son, that whosoever believeth in him should not perish, but have everlasting life." (John 3:16 KJV)

"But he was wounded for our transgressions, he was bruised for our iniquities: the chastisement of our peace was upon him; and with his stripes we are healed. - All we like sheep have gone astray; we have turned every one to his own way; and the LORD hath laid on him the iniquity of us all." (Isaiah 53:5,6 KJV)

Who his own self bare our sins in his own body on the tree, that we, being dead to sins, should live unto righteousness; by whose stripes ye were healed. For ye were as sheep going astray; but are now returned unto the Shepherd and Bishop of your souls (1 Peter 2:24, 25 KJV)

In this text Peter was then talking to new believers who were converted to Christianity after the resurrection of Jesus. Whether, Jews and or Gentiles, whosoever has accepted the sacrifice of Jesus Christ as their Savior who died on the cross at Calvary by the shading of his blood for the redemption of the soul of mankind, they are now set free indeed from the penalty of sin, and now receives life more abundantly. (1Tim.1:16 KJV)

MANKIND DISOBEYED GOD

What is sin? "lawlessness, Disobeying the law of God. Transgression of the law." All unrighteousness is sin." (1Jn.5:17 KJV)

God made mankind in His own image "And God said, Let us make man in our image, after our likeness: and let them have dominion over the fish of the sea, and over the fowl of the air, and over the cattle, and over all the earth, and over every creeping thing that creepeth upon the earth. So God created man in his own image, in the image of God created he him; male and female created he him. "(Gen.1:26,27 KJV) God placed mankind in this world without sin. Then, Adam disobeyed the commandment of God and ate from the tree of the knowledge of good and evil which God commanded him not to eat.

A time when mankind was truly obedient to God. Everything under the sun was under his dominion. There had never been a fallen leave from a tree. Nothing had ever died. No unpleasantness. Not even the prick of a sharp object, because there was no such thing until after mankind sinned.

"And the LORD God commanded the man, saying, Of every tree of the garden thou mayest freely eat: but of the tree of the knowledge of good and evil, thou shalt not eat of it: for in the day that thou eatest thereof thou shalt surely die." (Gen.2:16,17 KJV) The Devil-Satan who was cast out of heaven down to earth beguiled Adam's wife Eve and caused her to have eaten the fruit of the forbidden tree. She then gave the fruit to her husband Adam and he did eat.

An angel created by God known as Lucifer before mankind coveted the place of God. " How art thou fallen from heaven, O Lucifer, son of the morning! How art thou cut down to the ground, which didst weaken the nations! For thou art said in thine heart, I will ascend into heaven, I will exalt my throne above the stars of God: I will sit also upon the mount of the congregation, in the sides of the north:. I will ascend above the heights of the clouds: I will be like the most High." (Isa.14:12-14 KJV)

Now that angel is cursed.

"And the Lord God said unto the serpent, Because thou hast done this, thou art cursed above every beast of the field; upon thy belly shalt *thou* go, and dust shalt thou eat all the days of thy life: (Gen. 3:14 KJV). "And that great Dragon was cast out, that old serpent, called the Devil and Satan, which deceiveth the whole world, he was cast out into the earth, and his angels were cast out with him." (Rev 12:9 KJV)

Gen.3: 1-7 KJV reads: "Now the serpent was more subtil than any beast of the field which the LORD God had made. And he said unto the woman, Yea, hath God said, Ye shall not eat of every tree of the garden?, and the woman said unto the serpent: We may eat of the fruit of the trees of the garden, But of the fruit of the tree which is in the midst of the garden, God hath said, Ye shall not eat of it, neither shall ye touch it, less ye die. And the serpent said unto the woman, Ye shall not surely die. For God doth know that in the day ye eat thereof, then your eyes shall be opened, and ye shall be as gods, knowing good and evil. and when the woman saw that the tree was good for food, and that it was pleasant to the eyes, and a tree to be desired to make one wise, she took of the fruit thereof, and did eat and gave also unto her husband with her; and he did eat. and the eyes of them both were opened, and they knew that they were naked; and they sewed fig leaves together, and made themselves aprons."

The result of disobedience to God's command is sin. That's the effect of that which took place and the result thereof. By mankind being separated from God through disobedience we still have the effects until today. Example: Adam and Eve's eyes were opened to good and evil. They saw themselves now naked. Their reaction. They separated leaves from the fig tree to cover their nakedness. Adam and Eve tried to hide from God.

New thoughts entered their minds, unusual words uttered, destructive actions took place and ungodly results realized. Let us read what the Holy Bible says;

'And unto Adam He said,

"Because thou hast hearkened unto the voice of thy wife and hast eaten of the tree of which I commanded thee saying Thou shalt not eat of it: cursed [is] the ground for thy sake; in sorrow shalt thou eat [of] it all the days of thy life; Thorns also and thistles shall it bring forth to thee; and thou shalt eat the herb of the field; In the sweat of thy face shalt thou eat bread till thou return unto the ground for out of it wast thou taken: for dust thou [art], and unto dust shalt thou return." (Gen 3: 17-19 KJV).

THE MESSIAH

Here comes "Jesus Christ the Living Word" approximately 4000 years latter. "He who was predestined to be the redeemer of mankind, even before the foundation of the world. "According as he hath chosen us in him before the foundation of the world, that we should be holy and without blame before him in love: Having predestined us unto the adoption of children by Jesus Christ to himself, according to the good pleasure of his will." (Eph 1: 4,5 KJV).

Jesus, in his original state, before he was manifested to us in the flesh and came and lived among men He went to the rescue of mankind. Here God sought Adam and asked His created being "Adam where art thou." The same God who created us came in search of Adam and Eve and He found our first parents covered with leaves. (Gen. 3:8 KJV)

"Unto Adam also and to his wife did the Lord God make coats of skins, and clothed them." (Gen.3:21 KJV) Where those skins came from? Was blood shed? Was that an evidence of things to come? For instance, what the Savior would do for the redemption of mankind on Calvary's cross?

Well, years later, St. Luke wrote these verses " And the angel said unto them, Fear not: for, behold, I bring you good tidings of great joy, which shall be to all people.

For unto you is born this day in the city of David a Savior who is Christ the Lord." (Lk.2:10,11KJV)

The prophecies of Isaiah from many years prior to Jesus' birth was fulfilled. The book of Isaiah chapter 53 gives prophetic outline of the life of the Messiah many years before he came.

I do hope you have a copy of the Holy Bible, if you do please read that chapter (Isaiah 53). If you do not have a Bible, and you would like to have one, please write and make your request known to us .

Here, Jn. 3:16 KJV said: "For God so loved the world, that he gave his only begotten Son, that whosoever believeth in him should not perish, but have everlasting life." It speaks of God's Love, His Gift, the sacrifice for our redemption.

If we accept him as he is, the Son of God,. the Savior of mankind, we will receive, a benefit - everlasting life. This "life" mankind lost (separation from God) when he disobeyed the command of God and ate the fruit.

God the Almighty through his love, at the beginning he created heaven and earth and we note that in creating all things, He included mankind within the six literal days. And on the seventh-day God rested and mankind learned more about God's love. "And on the seventh-day God ended his work which he had made; and he rested on the seventh -day from all his work which he had made. And God blessed the seventh day, and sanctified it: because that in it he had rested from all his work which God created and made." (Gen. 2:2,3 KJV)

Continuing about the Messiah as human-being. He came through the Jewish nation. A young woman named Mary gave birth to this male child and his name was Jesus. He the Savior of the world was predestined to come to save his people from their sins. (Matt.1:21 KJV) The Jewish nation was selected and blessed through Abraham to bring blessings to all mankind. When one individually accepts the Christian teachings of this Savior Jesus Christ by repentance- turning away from doing wrong and then confesses his sins directly to Jesus "by faith," Jesus will forgive him or her.

1 John 1:9 KJV) said "If we confess our sins, He is faithful and just to forgive us our sins, and cleanse us from all unrighteousness." The result, is that,you will receive a new life known as "everlasting Life". With the in-dwelling of the Holy Spirit, you will think, speak, and act differently. He will teach you all truth and direct your path whereby you will have a new life-style.

In Gen.12: 2-5 KJV) we read that God called a man named Abram and told him to go to a place where God would show him. There God would make a great nation, He would bless him, make his name great, and would make this Abram a blessing. This blessing was so tremendous that it is said of God to this man Abram

"I will bless them that bless thee and curse them that curseth thee." (Gen.12:2-3 KJV) That is an agreement or covenant God made with him. Through the blessing of this man came forth Jesus the Messiah thou many years after, who was in the lineage of David. David was born after Abram's son Isaac and his grand-son Jacob. Jacob, his name was changed from Jacob to Israel (Gen. 32:28 KJV.)

From Jacob came a nation of twelve tribes according to the names of his sons. Now the offspring of Jacob multiplied over the years, and were called children of Israel.

Judah was the fourth son of Israel ancestors to David . The linage in which Jesus was born according to the prophecy "And Joseph also went up from Galilee, out of the city of Nazareth, into Judea, unto the city of David, which is called Bethlehem; (because he was of the house and lineage of David:) For unto you is born this day in the city of David a Savior, which is Christ the Lord." (LK.2:4,11 KJV)

The genealogy of Jesus in part was recorded in scripture.

"Now these are the generations of Pherez: Pharez begat Hezron, And Hezron begat Ram, and Ram begat Amminadab, And Amminadab begat Nahshon, And Nahshon begat Salmon, And Salmon begat Boaz, and Boaz begat Obed, And Obed begat Jesse, and Jesse begat David. (Ruth 4:18-22 KJV) And Eliud begat

Eleazar; and Eleazar begat Matthan; and Matthan begat Jacob; and Jacob begat Joseph the husband of Mary of whom was born Jesus who is called Christ" (Matt 1:15,16 KJV)

Jesus now began his earthly public ministry.

"And Jesus himself began to be about thirty years of age, being (as was supposed) the son of Joseph, who was the son of Heli". (Luke 3:23, 38.KJV) A descendant from Adam who was the created son of God. Three and one-half years later after he began his earthly ministry he was crucified.

Dan.9: 26 KJV) makes it plain that within the last week or seven years the Messiah would be cut off, not for himself. Just as prophesied, midst of the last seven years of the four hundred and ninety years he was crucified as the lamb slain being the redeeming sacrifice for the soul of man. The Antitype of the sacrificial type-of-system that the nation of Israel observed as Passover from the preparing to cross over the Jordon river out from under the bondage of Egypt and also the atonement for sins that were committed throughout the year on the day of atonement, e.g. Killing a lamb or goat etc. as a sacrifice was not necessary after the crucifixion of Jesus on the cross.

"It is said and I will pour upon the house of David, and upon the inhabitants of Jerusalem, the spirit of grace and of supplication; and they shall look upon me whom they have pierced, and they shall mourn of him, as one moureth for his own son, and shall be in bitterness for him, as one that is in bitterness for his firstborn". (Zec.12:10 KJV)

In 34 A.D the end of the four hundred and ninety years (490) which was determined upon the Jews as told to Daniel, came to an end as signified by the stoning of Stephen to death. The first Christian Martyr.

During Jesus' earthly ministry when He met the woman of Samaria at Jacob's Well, he emphasized that he was the Messiah. Notice the dialogue between them. Jesus asked her for a drink of water and they proceeded in the conversation where Jesus brought to her attention some of her previous activities in life.

"The woman saith unto him, I know that messias. cometh, which is called Christ: when he is come, he will tell us all things." 'Jesus said unto her, I that speaketh unto you am He.' " (John 4:25, 26 KJV) Here Jesus expressly told the Samaritan woman who He was, the Messiah, the Anointed One.

The joyous thing about this, the Messiah prophesied in scripture was the same Jesus who declared to the woman at the well, "whosoever drinketh of the water that I shall give him shall never thirst: but the water that I give him shall be in him a well of water springing up into everlasting life." (Jn. 4:14 KJV)

That same Jesus is able to give you the same gift (s) today if you believe and accept the fact that he is the Son of God, the spotless lamb of God. He who shed his blood on Calvary's cross for our redemption. The propitiation/payment for our reconciliation. He is The Messiah.

"Whosoever drinketh of the water that I shall give him shall never thirst: but the water that I give him shall be in him a well of water springing up into everlasting life." (Jn .4.14 KJV)

'Whosoever believes and accepts Him, they will never have to suffer the agony of hell. He likewise promised that He will come again to take us from this world of ungodly activities to a mansion in his Father's house. To signify this promise there were two men Elijah a prophet of God who never experienced death but was translated from earth to heaven. (2 kgs.2:11KJV) Moses, who had died on mount Nebo." (Deu.32:49,50 and 34:1-5 KJV). Those two men appeared to be with Jesus on the mount of Transfiguration." "And there appeared to them Elijah with Moses, and they were talking with Jesus." (Mk. 9:4. KJV) You also can speak directly to Jesus Christ as your Savior and Lord today.

TIME PROPHECY

Some very significant prophetic messages came to Daniel. Daniel one who was captured by Nebuchadnezzar out of Jerusalem and then became a Prophet of God. He lived in Babylon under the rule of Nebuchadnezzar the King of Babylon. (Dan.1;1 KJV)

The following is a brief interpretation of that prophecy. The prophecy began with the rebuilding of Jerusalem about 457BC and ended in 34AD when Stephen, the first Christian martyr was stoned to death. That year marked the end of the four hundred and ninety (490) years allotted to the Jewish Nation

Another significant thing you should know. In this prophecy a day equals one year. "After the number of the days in which ye searched the land, [even] forty days, each day for a year, shall ye bear your iniquities, [even] forty years, and ye shall know my breach of promise" (Numbers 14:34 KJV) Also.

"And when thou hast accomplished them, lie again on thy right side, and thou shalt bear the iniquity of the house of Judah forty days: I have appointed thee each day for a year." (Ezl.4:6 KJV)

This prophetic message given to Daniel would also verify who was the Messiah and much more to the end of the world.

The prophetic message reads, "Seventy weeks are determined upon thy people and upon thy holy city, to finish the transgression, and to make an end of sins, and to make reconciliation for iniquity, and to bring in everlasting righteousness, and to seal up the vision and prophecy, and to anoint the most Holy. Know therefore and understand, that from the going forth of the commandment to restore and to build Jerusalem unto the Messiah the Prince shall be seven weeks, and threescore and two weeks: the street shall be built again, and the wall, even in troublous times. And after threescore and two weeks shall Messiah be cut off, but not for himself: and the people of the prince that shall come shall destroy the city and the sanctuary; and the end thereof shall be with a flood, and unto the end of the war desolations are determined. And he shall confirm the covenant with many for one week: and in the midst of the week he shall cause the sacrifice and the oblation to cease, and for the overspreading of abominations he shall make it desolate, even until the consummation, and that determined shall be poured upon the desolate." (Dan. 9:24-27 KJV)

Dan.9:24 **Seventy weeks**: a certain period of time set for thy People and upon thy holy city which was Jerusalem.

2. **Make an end of sins**. The payment made by the Blood-Life of Jesus Christ the spotless, Holy Lamb of God on the cross at Calvary. Therefore, the sacrificial system that was in place led by the Jewish Nation would

not be in effect any-more. For instance, on the day of atonement a lamb was killed by the shedding of it's blood as a type of what the Savior would do for the redemption of mankind. As it is known, that was done at Calvary on the cross. "But with the precious blood of Christ, as of a lamb without blemish and without spot:" (1 Pet.1:19 KJV)

3. **Make reconciliation for iniquity**. By his vicarious sacrifice on Calvary Christ provided reconciliation for all who accept his sacrifice. <u>Vol.4 SDA bible commentary pg 852.</u>

4. **Bring in everlasting righteousness**: Christ did not come to earth simply to provide for the blotting out of sin. He came to reconciled man to God. He came so that it might be possible to impute and to impart His righteousness to the penitent sinner.When men accept Him, He bestows on them the robe of His righteousness, and they stand in God presence as though they never sinned.

<u>vol. 4 SDA bible commentary pg. 852.</u>

"Know therefore and understand, that from the going forth of the commandment to restore and rebuild Jerusalem unto the Messiah the Prince shall be seven weeks, and threescore and two weeks: the street shall be built again, and the wall, even in troublous times." (Dan.9:25 KJV)

"Though the time frame was in a different format. Specific instructions were given. Here we saw the prophesy of Jeremiah really comes to its fulfillment. For thus saith the LORD, "That after seventy years be accomplished at Babylon I will visit you, and perform my good word toward you, in causing you to return to this place. For I know the thoughts that I think towards you, saith the LORD, thoughts of peace and not of evil, to give you and expected end." (Jer. 29:10-11KJV)

V26: After the number of 69 weeks or 483 days-years the Messiah the Prince would be cut off, but not for himself; Then the people of the prince that shall come shall destroy the City and sanctuary: (Dan. 9:26 KJV)

V27: The last of the seventy weeks. In the midst of this seventieth week he the Messiah shall cause the sacrifice and the oblation to cease…

If this was literally seventy weeks it would equal one year four months and two weeks. The time period from the giving of the command to the birth of Jesus would be long gone. The public ministry of Jesus was over three and one half years.

The first 7 weeks 7x7 equals 49 days. In prophecy days equal years as pointed out earlier. In the next 62 weeks equals 434 days which equals 434 years..

Therefore 7+62 = 69 wks or   483 yrs

The 70th wk equal   7 yrs split in two halves

                         3.5 mid wk Jesus crucified.

                         3.5 yrs later Stephen stoned

Total amount of years   490yrs From 458/7 B.C.-33/4 A.D.

A quick observation of this time frame

457BC_____A.D_27_____31/AD_____34AD

Command given   Jesus baptized in Jordon   crucified   Stephen stoned

In 457 B.C Ezra, priest and scribe in Babylon received a command from Artarxerxes, king of Persia (Iran) to go and restore and rebuild

Jerusalem. You may read the letter of authorization at (Ezra 7:11-26 KJV).

This prophecy was prophesied over 400 years before the birth of Jesus.

BAPTISM

We have drawn to your attention some points relating to the name Jesus. The background in giving names, especially in Bible times. The name Jesus and its meaning. Undoubtedly this name is given for its true meaning. Jehovah is Salvation.

As we have seen that Peter openly declared that this Jesus which was rejected by those leaders and people was truly our Messiah, Savior and Lord. Through Him salvation comes. He must be revered as Savior and Lord . In the book of Matthew we saw that after the resurrection of Jesus he gave the command of baptism in the commemorative name of the Godhead, from an instructional point-of-view, knowing, he was a teacher (Jn. 3:2, mk. 12:14 KJV) and from a student's point-of-view (Heb. 5:8 KJV) who had been the first of his class he gave a valedictory command at this the end of his physical earthly ministry. We are sanctioned to minister on behalf of the Three-in-One -The Godhead. In an authoritative way. "And Jesus came and spake unto them, saying, All power is given unto me in heaven and in earth. Go ye therefore, and teach all nations, baptizing them in the name of the Father, and of the Son, and of the Holy Ghost: Teaching them to observe all things whatsoever I have commanded you: and, lo, I am with you always, even unto the end of the world. Amen." (Matt.28:18-20 KJV)

In the book of Mark it is also said: "And he said unto them, Go ye into all the world, and preach the gospel to every creature. He that believeth and is baptized shall be saved; but he that believeth not shall be damned. And these signs shall follow them that believe; In my name shall they cast out devils; they shall speak with new tongues; They shall take up serpents; and if they drink any deadly thing, it shall not hurt them; they shall lay hands on the sick, and they shall recover." *(*Mark16:15-18 KJV)

At this point, do you know that one of the outward signs of water baptism is to show that whoever received it has now devote himself or herself to the service of God?

Consider the message of John in the Book of Revelation:

And I saw another angel fly in the midst of heaven, having the everlasting gospel to preach unto them that dwell on the earth, and to every nation, and kindred, and tongue, and people, Saying with a loud voice, Fear God, and give glory to him; for the hour of his judgment is come: and worship him that made heaven, and earth, and the sea, and the fountains of waters.

And there followed another angel, saying, Babylon is fallen, is fallen, that great city, because she made all nations drink of the wine of the wrath of her fornication.

And the third angel followed them, saying with a loud voice, If any man worship the beast and his image, and receive his mark in his forehead, or in his hand, The same shall drink of the wine of the wrath of God, which is poured out without mixture into the cup of his indignation; and he shall be tormented with fire and brimstone in the presence of the holy angels, and in the presence of the Lamb: And the smoke of their torment ascendeth up for ever and ever: and they have no rest day nor night, who worship the beast and his image, and whosoever receiveth the mark of his name. Here is the patience of the saints: here are they that keep the commandments of God, and the faith of Jesus." (Rev. 14:6-12 KJV)

Would you be willing to follow Jesus as your Savior and Lord? _____

If yes is your answer

Please pray: Dear Jesus I believe you are the Son of God. You paid for my redemption at Calvary. Please forgive me of my sins-unrighteousness and help me to serve you daily amen.

I pray to God that the true meaning of reading this booklet will be realized in your acceptance of Jesus Christ as your Savior and Lord. I pray that the Holy Spirit will permeate your soul and you will be convicted of your unrighteousness and as you confess your faults to the Savior, who is the Messiah, your fate will be assured as you exercise your faith in him while he awaits you in that place he has gone to prepare, with wide open arms full of love, through his mercy and grace which he demonstrated at Calvary on the cross.

The writer, being led to write this book for evangelism, shall appreciate your response in comments and support to help this mission to distribute books to various parts of the world.

You could receive a copy of the Holy Bible.

Please allow God to use you to witness to others even through your support of this book.

A dedicated attendant to the Methodist Church. After a while, I was sent off to school in the United States of America. My major was Accounting and Marketing. Employment, was with The Bank of the Commonwealth Downtown Detroit. Then off to Jamaica where I worked for The Jamaica Gleaner Company. Soon I migrate to Canada and began an Accounting & Tax Services firm.

I am now married to Delores. We have two children, and as of now, three grandchildren.

HEGNAL S. DAWSON

Re: The Messiah Has Risen

P.O. Box 77073

Woodbridge Ontario L4L 9S3

sunbeam.sd@gmail.com

http://www.sunbeam77.com

NOTES

NOTES

NOTES